Fairy Poems

Clare Bevan lives in a cobwebby house with her husband, Martin, her son, Ben, and a family of stick insects. She used to be a teacher, but now she spends most of her time writing poems. Her favourite hobbies are acting, wearing hats and riding around her village on a big, purple tricycle.

Lara Jones lives in a tiny cottage, by a misty hill, with her husband, Shaun. She likes painting pictures, eating Marmite on toast, and dreaming out of the window.

D1465363

Fairy Poems

By Clare Bevan

Illustrated by Lara Jones

MACMILLAN CHILDREN'S BOOKS

*Dedicated to YOU, my reader – may there
always be a little magic in your life. And also
to Rachel, my very own Fairy Godmother.*

First published 2004 by Macmillan Children's Books
a division of Macmillan Publishers Limited
20 New Wharf Road, London N1 9RR
Basingstoke and Oxford
www.panmacmillan.com

Associated companies throughout the world

ISBN 0 330 43352 0

5 7 9 8 6 4

A CIP catalogue record for this book is available from
the British Library.

Typeset by Nigel Hazle
Printed and bound in Great Britain by Mackays of Chatham plc, Kent

Contents

A Bedtime Rhyme for Young Fairies

Whispered to Clare Bevan in a dream

One tired fairy,
Two folded wings,
Three magic wishes,
Four daisy rings,
Five moonlight dancers,
Six starlight spells,
Seven hidden treasures,
Eight silver bells,
Nine secret doorways,
Ten keys to keep,
And one little fairy
Fast asleep.

Fairy Names

*When Clare found this poem, all the names had
been crossed out . . . except for one!*

What shall we call the Fairy Child?

Mouse-Fur? Cat's Purr?
Weasel-Wild?

Bat-Wing? Bee-Sting?
Shining River?
Snakebite? Starlight?
Stone? Or Shiver?

Acorn? Frogspawn?
Golden Tree?
Snowflake? Daybreak?
Stormy Sea?

Snail-Shell? Harebell?
Scarlet Flame?

How shall we choose the Fairy's name?

A Flutter of Fairies

Collected by Clare

A flutter of fairies.
A whisper of wings.
A shiver of cobwebs.
A spangle of rings.
A canter of horse flies.
A rumble of bees.
A splatter of frogs.
A city of trees.
A village of toadstools,
An ocean of ponds.
A procession of snails.
A sparkle of wands.
A glimmer of glow-worms.
A treasure of dew.
A shower of wishes
For me. And for you.

A Fairy Gift Catalogue

Found inside a flowerpot

From The Fairies' Catalogue
    You can choose –

Foxglove hats,
Frogskin shoes,
Stripy socks
To warm your knees,
(Made from fur
Of bumblebees.)
Special slippers,
Light and strong,
To dance on moonbeams
All night long.

Treetop rides,
Cobweb swings,
Bouncy mushrooms,
Stars on strings,
Rocking horseflies,
Bugs to hug,
Snails on wheels,
A small, pet slug.

Conker chairs and
Toadstool tables
Racing mice in
Mossy stables,
Best of all
The gift I'd like –
A wand made from
A hedgehog spike.

A Fairy Recipe

Found inside an empty snail shell

YOU WILL NEED:

A nutshell of honey,
A plain, white flower,
A butterfly's egg,
The mist from a shower,
The glint of a rainbow,
The gleam of a fish,
The hum of a bumblebee
Mixed with a wish.

METHOD:

Stir it and taste
With a secretive spoon,
Heat very gently
Under the moon,
Cool it with snowflakes,
Sprinkle with frost,
Slice with a dagger
Carelessly lost.

To serve:

Wait for the beat
Of a dragonfly's wing
Place in a casket
Owned by a king,
Leave by the shore
Of a whispering lake –

Now you have made me
A REAL fairy cake.

Letters

Found under a pillow

Dear Tooth Fairy,

I really don't
Believe in you,
But here's my tooth
(In case you're true.)

PS And IF you visit,
Can you say
Why you steal
My teeth away?

Dear Tooth Giver,

I DO take teeth,
But NEVER steal –
So here's a coin
To prove I'm real.

I use the teeth
To build tall towers
Where fairies learn
Their magic powers.

PS

I think you have
A lovely smile.
Not bad . . .
For a crocodile.

9

The Fairy King

Overheard by Clare

The Fairy King
is armed with the sting
Of a wasp, and a bramble spear.

He rides the sky
On a dragonfly,
And his eyes are cold and clear.

He'll fight the cat
Or a snag-toothed rat,
He'll see them off with a sneer,

And he prowls the wood
As a great king should,
With weasel and snake and deer.

But he's never seen
In his cloak of green
When you or I draw near.

A School Report

From the Hollow Tree Charm School for Fairy Children. Hidden inside Clare's hollow tree

Name: F. Thunderfoot

Subject – Dancing:

Fairy Thunderfoot always does her best.
She has tried VERY hard
To balance on a moonbeam,
To spin on the top of a pin,
To skip in neat circles,
But, sadly, she failed her Dancing Test
When she toppled off her toadstool.

Subject – Cooking:

Fairy Thunderfoot always does her best.
She has tried VERY hard
Not to lick her silver spoon,
Not to spill her fairy dust,
Not to stir her wand QUITE so fast,
But, sadly, she failed her Fairy Cake Test
When she accidentally ate them all.

Subject – Tooth-Finding:

Fairy Thunderfoot always does her best.
She has tried VERY hard
To tiptoe round rooms without giggling,
To peep under pillows without sneezing,
To count shiny coins without dropping
    them,
But, sadly, she failed her Tooth Fairy Test
When she sat on a squeaky teddy bear.

Subject – Spelling and Sparkling:

Fairy Thunderfoot always does her best.
She has tried VERY hard
To grant wishes for worried children,
To weave dreams for sleepy children,
To cast cheerful spells for sad children,
And, happily, she has passed her Fairy
    Godmother Test
With a shower of golden stars.

Fairy Ring

Clare got very dizzy when she read this poem

Find the centre, bow and then Take my hand and START AGAIN! Spiral past the hollow tree, Twirl and swirl and swiftly spin Up and down and out and in, follow me, Clever Queen and frisky King, Party fairies, the daisy ring, Dance around

The Mouse-Rider's Rap

This mouse-race was secretly watched by Clare

Harness your mouse,
And cling to his fur,
Wait for the sound
Of the tomcat's purr,
Then gallop away
Under the trees,
Leap over the molehills
Faster than fleas,
Swerve down the track
Where a cat can't follow,
Twist and turn to
The hidden hollow,
Skid and scramble
Around the lawn,
Jump the nettles
And dodge the yawn
Of the sleeping dog
With his yellow fangs,
Cross the line
As the harebell clangs,

Take a bow
When the dawn comes up,
Proudly hold
The Acorn Cup,
Pat your mouse
And serve his dinner –
That's the way
To be a WINNER.

The Spider

This poem was pinned to a tiny grave under Clare's hazel tree

The fairy child loved her spider.

Even when it grew fat
And grey and old,
She would comb its warm fur
With a hazel twig
And take it for slow walks
On its silky lead.

Sometimes it played cat-cradles with her
But more often it wove hammocks
Amongst the long grasses
And they swung together under friendly
    trees.

When it died,
Her mother bought her a money spider
Who scuttled and tumbled to make her
    smile.
But it wasn't the same,
And still, when she curls up to sleep
In the lonely dawn,
She murmurs her old spider's name.

The Fairy Godmother

*Written in purple ink, and pushed under
Clare's door*

The Fairy Godmother looks down
At her wide, purple skirts
And they seem faded now.
Her wand needs a new handle,
And her dancing slippers
Have started to creak.

When she peeps through windows,
The children play with enchanted toys
In silver boxes
That flash and flicker
And teach them how to frown.
The new magic troubles her.

But all the same,
Her spells fly faster than any spaceship,
Her three wishes can beat any computer
    game,
And her gift of happiness is still more
    precious
Than all the presents on Earth.

21

The New Fairy Godmother

*Written in glittery ink, and pushed under
Clare's door*

The New Fairy Godmother's having fun,
  Casting spells for EVERYONE.

    The giant has a teddy bear
    Extra big.
    The wolf has a cosy house
    Built for a pig.
    The princess is married to
    A handsome frog.
    The three blind mice
    Have a helpful dog.
    The witch has a speedboat.
    Her cat has new boots.
    The duck and the penguin

Have diving suits.
The rabbit has a roar.
The fish has a bark.
The mole has a torch
To shine in the dark.
The cow has a rocket.
The spoon has a dish.
And you? Close your eyes.
Make your own, special wish.

The new Fairy Godmother's having fun,
Casting spells for EVERYONE.

The Magic Wand

Found amongst a clump of dandelions, by Clare

Sparkle,
Shimmer,
Glitter
Gleam,
Scatter starlight on a stream,
Golden beetle, silver fishes,
Hear my – Spell and
Grant my – Wishes.

Wave
The
Wand
And
Twist
And
Spin
Now
The
Magic
Can
B
E
G
I
N

If You Hear . . .

A poem murmured in Clare's ear

If you think you hear a rustle
In the grasses by your door,
If you spot a tiny footprint
In the dust upon your floor,
If you see a baby sleeping
In the petals of a rose,
If you peer inside a mouse hole
And a lantern softly glows,
If your tooth, so small and precious
Is collected in the night,
Then perhaps you'll find the doorway
To the magic Land of Light.

A Fairy Tale

Told to Clare by her grandmother

My grandmother's grandmother,
(So it is said)
Was only six
When she jumped from her bed,
And was whirled away
On a winter dawn
As the north wind swept
The frosty lawn.

My grandmother's grandmother,
(So they say)
Came skipping home
One summer's day.
Her hair was silver,
Her eyes were wild,
And she spoke of life
As a fairy child.

My grandmother's grandmother,
(So they sing)
Wore a brooch as blue
As a beetle's wing.
She kept a slipper
Made from glass,
And she slept in a nest
Of tangled grass.

My grandmother's grandmother,
(So it is told)
Dreamed fairy dreams
When she grew old.
Her heart was as light
As a robin's feather,
And one warm night
She vanished forever.

The Fairy Rule Book

This little book was tucked inside Clare's pencil box

1. Do not tease the Badger.
   (She will bite you.)
2. Do not hunt the Fieldmouse.
   (He will fight you.)
3. Never tickle Magpies.
   (They will snatch you.)
4. Never talk to Humans.
   (They will catch you.)

5. Always dance by Moonlight.
   (It will glisten.)
6. Always trust the Barn Owl.
   (She will listen.)
7. Wrap your wand in Starshine.
   (It will shimmer.)
8. Treat your Glow-Worm kindly.
   (It will glimmer.)

9. Clean your Magic Mirror.
   (It will guide you.)
10. Wear your Cloak of Shadows.
    (It will hide you.)
11. Read your Secret Spell Book.
    (Read it nightly.)
12. Cast your Charms with Joy.
    (And cast them lightly.)

IF YOU KEEP THESE FAIRY RULES
YOU'LL SPARKLE BRIGHTLY.

The Bad Fairy

Clare found a drawing of the bad fairy pinned to her bird table

Her dress is stitched with cobwebs
Her wings are poison-green,
She frightens fairy children
Once a year, at Hallowe'en,
Her eyes are hard as jewels,
And her smile is rarely seen.

Her wand is one, thin whisker
From a cruel, ginger cat,
She wears a holly helmet,
She rides a giant rat,
But her heart is lost and lonely –
I'm very sure of that.

Fairy Gifts

For all sorts of special days.
Clare would love to find a fairy gift

Fairies give AMAZING gifts
To babies and to brides.
Happy spells
In walnut shells,
Or golden pumpkin rides.

Fairies give AMAZING gifts
To story girls and boys.
A talking fish,
A magic dish
A castle FULL of toys.

Fairies give AMAZING gifts,
I hope they'll bring to you
A birthday cake
With power to make
Your secret wish comes true.

*Clare caught this in a shower
of autumn leaves*

Invitation to the Fairy Queen's Ball

*The Fairy Queen invites us ALL
To the Fairy Wood for the Fairy Ball.*

*We'll sew our skirts with spidery care,
We'll choose a necklace old and rare,
We'll skip along the royal stair
In glassy slippers, light as air.*

*But whatever we do, and whatever we wear,
Our Queen will be the loveliest there,
With her gown so plain and her feet so bare,
And a circle of daisies in her hair.*

Fairy Puzzle

*Clare once knew the answer, but she has
forgotten it*

My First is in FROST but not in ICE,
My Second's in MOLE but not in MICE,
My Third's in TREASURE but not in
   DISH,
My Fourth is in WAND but not in WISH,
My Fifth is in SNAKE and also SNAIL,
My Sixth is in BOAT but not in SAIL,
My Seventh's in OWL and ROBIN too,
My Eighth's in RAINBOW but not in
   BLUE,
My Last is in SLIPPERS but not in SHOES,
My Whole is a Home the fairies choose.

My answer's a TOADSTOOL, red and white,
Where windows gleam at dead of night.

The Barn Owl

Clare found this poem carved into an old tree stump

The Barn Owl isn't
As wise as you think,
With her spooky hoot
And her sleepy wink.

But we don't much care,
And we don't much mind –
Her wings are warm
And her heart is kind.

35

Scribble

This poem was written in silver along Clare's front path

Moth-Wing's parents gave him
A small and spotty slug.
It wasn't what he wanted.
It wasn't fun to hug.

His friends had handsome beetles,
Or horseflies they could ride,
But Moth-Wing's pet was slimy
(Which rather hurt his pride.)

One early summer morning,
In the early summer haze,
Moth-Wing saw the shimmer
Of a MASSIVE silver maze.

Silver lines were swirling
From the centre to the start –
The garden had been turned into
A silver work of art.

The patterns twirled and twinkled
Where the earth was freshly dug,
And in the middle of it all . . .
Sat Moth-Wing's busy slug.

His pet was small and spotty.
It wasn't fun to touch,
But Moth-Wing called it "SCRIBBLE"
And he loved it VERY much.

The Tricky Fairy

This Puzzle Poem gave Clare a headache

So – are all fairies good?
Not all. And not ME.
Am I keen to cause trouble?
Keen as can be!
Every dusk. Every dawn.
By night, and by day
I'm ready to trick and
To tease and to play . . .
Even my NAME is hidden away!

(Has the fairy won this game?
Or can you spot her naughty name?)

Answer: The tricky Fairy's name is SNAKE BITE
– Read DOWN the page, not left to right.

Fairy Artists

This poem was written in the frost on Clare's car

The Autumn Fairy dips her wand
In colours of fire.
She changes the dark, dusty leaves
Of the Summer trees
Into golden coins
That sparkle and scatter
Like a pirate's treasure
Under the scarlet sky.

The Frost Fairy tickles the air
With her icicle wand
And covers the cold fingers
Of Winter trees
With glittering white gloves,
She decorates the sleeping cars
With feathers and sugar stars,
And she hangs Christmas tinsel
From every leaky drainpipe.

The Autumn Fairy is an artist,
But the Frost Fairy
Is a spinner of dreams.

Tooth Fairies Wanted

This poem was fixed to Clare's bedroom window

TOOTH FAIRIES WANTED.
Must be brave,
Must have deep blue
Wands to wave,
Must be quick and,
Must be clever,
Must not wake
A human EVER!

Must like danger,
Must be strong,
(Human teeth are
Large and long.)
Must be good at
Finding things.
Must have dark
And silent wings.

Must not fear
The dog or cat,
Must not mind
A top-floor flat.
Must know how
To read and write
Notes – WITHOUT
A glow-worm's light.

Must not play
With children's toys.
(Cars and bears
Can make a noise.)
Must enjoy
Exciting flights,
Nasty scares and
Awful frights.

If you have the
Skills we need,
(Courage, quietness
And speed,)
Join our Midnight
Team today . . .
Ring our bell
And flap this way.

PS   We will give our
     New Collectors
     Bags of coins
     And Tooth Detectors.

A Sleepy Story

This poem was written in the back of Clare's fairy-tale book

The Tooth Fairy followed her Sky Map
Over the snowy mountains,
Over the spooky forest,
Over the tangled brambles,
To the Palace of Sorrow.

She flew softly, softly past
The soldiers with their rusty axes.
She flew softly, softly through
The grey gates with their dusty hinges.
She flew softly, softly along
The sad corridors with their musty rugs.

But when she tiptoed around
The last creaky door,
When she heard the horrible guard dog
Snuffle and snore,
When she touched his yellow tooth
On the stony floor,
She whispered to herself,
"Everyone, from the cook
To the King
And the tiniest kitchen fly
Is fast asleep."

Then she laughed OUT LOUD!
She clattered up and down the spiral stairs,
She rattled the bars of the highest win-
dows,
She jumped on the Sleeping Beauty's big,
bouncy bed,
She shouted at the giant spiders,
She danced along the piano keys,
She slid down a hundred squeaky banisters,
And she flapped NOISILY all the way
home,

Nobody saw her, of course.
Only the Princess dreamed of wands and
wishes,
And a lonely Prince
(Who was cutting a path through the rose
bushes)
Thought he heard someone singing
Just above his head.

The Fairies of the Sea

*When Clare held a shell to her ear, she heard
this song*

No bats for us – but flying fishes,
Swooping where the seaweed swishes . . .
Here we grant our Deep Sea Wishes.

No homes for us – but booming shells,
Sunken wrecks and broken bells . . .
Here we weave our Deep Sea Spells.

No trees for us – but coral flowers,
Bright-blue forests, twisted towers . . .
Here we learn our Deep Sea Powers.

No birds for us – but singing whales,
Far below the swan-white sails . . .
Here we tell our Deep Sea Tales.

The Christmas Fairy's Song

This poem was found in Clare's Christmas stocking

When you plant your Christmas tree,
Decorate it lovingly,
Pin each shining star with care –
I'll be hiding. I'll be there.

When you twist your tinsel strands,
Sprinkle glitter from your hands,
Comb the angel's silky hair –
I'll be watching. I'll be there.

When you find, on Christmas Day,
Bulgy stockings, games to play,
Books and toys and sweets to share –
I'll be dancing. I'll be there.

When you wonder what, or who
Made your secret wish come true,
When Christmas magic fills the air –
I'll be smiling. I'll be there.

A Dress Design for the Christmas Fairy

This poem was found under Clare's Christmas tree

Squirrel-nest skirts,
Holly-berry trim,
Pine-needle coronet,
(Frost round the brim.)

Ivy-leaf cloak and
Beetle-shell shoes,
Thistle-fluff mittens,
(Too warm to lose.)

Goose-down jumper,
Lambswool tights,
Robin-feather scarf,
(For snowy nights.)

Wear with a smile
And whirl away
To sail all night
On Santa's sleigh.

The Year We Lost Our Christmas Fairy

Clare found this poem in a box of Christmas decorations

We searched the box of tinsel,
We peered around inside,
But we couldn't find our fairy
However hard we tried.

We made a star of cardboard
To sparkle in her place,
But our little tree looked lonely
Without her friendly face.

Next morning, very early,
We crept downstairs to see
If Santa Claus had hidden
Any presents by the tree.

And there we saw our fairy
Smiling down at us once more,
But lovelier than ever
In the brand-new dress she wore.

We don't know how she got there.
We don't know where she'd been.
But we keep her like a treasure
And we treat her like a queen.

Fairy Games

This poem was found in a box of wooden skittles

What are the games that fairies play?

Knock-Down-Dormouse. Jump On The Jay.
Hunt The Hazelnut. Caterpillar Catch.
Ring-A-Ring-A-Bluebell. Squirrel-Tail Snatch.
Centipede Races. Snowberry Ball.

Hedgehog Hoop-La. Spider-Up-The-Wall.
North Wind Draughts and Greenfly Guess.
High-Sky Hockey. Grasshopper Chess.
Leaf-Board Sailing. Leap The Frog.
Fight With A Feather. Fall Off A Log.
Stick-Stone Skittles. Hide In The Hay.

These are the games that fairies play.

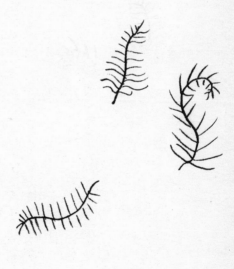

At the Fairy Flying School

This poem was fixed to the climbing frame in Clare's garden

At the Fairy Flying School

Some are clumsy,
Some are cool,
Some can dive
And loop-the-loop,
Some have wings
That dent and droop.

Some swoop higher
Than the larks,
Some crash-land
In clouds of sparks.
Some can spiral,
Some feel dizzy,
Some flap home
With hair all frizzy.

Some show off
And fool around,
Some can hardly
Leave the ground,
Some are braver
Than the rest
But ALL of them
Must take the test.

*(And if they flutter hard, and try –
ALL of them will learn to fly.)*

At the Fairy Shoe Shop

This poem was tucked inside one of Clare's best boots

Which shoes will YOU choose?
Hunting boots with spurs?
Cosy winter slippers
Lined with insect furs?

Crystal shoes for dreamers?
Acorn clogs for walkers?
Feathered heels for flyers?
Silent soles for talkers?

Sandals laced with grasses?
Trainers spiked or spiny?
Wellies made from fish-scales,
Waterproof and shiny?

Giant shoes with windows,
Stairs and rooms and doors?
Special stripy bedsocks
Shaped like badger paws?

Which shoes will YOU choose?
Just ONE wish to pay . . .
Guaranteed to last you
A whole year – and a day!

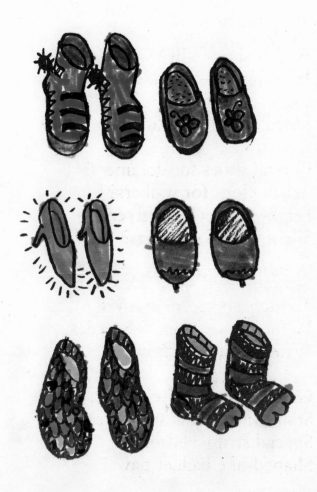

Houses for Sale!

*Clare found this noticeboard
propped against her wheelbarrow*

Houses for sale!
Houses for sale!

A snail-shell home
(Without the snail.)
A smart new toadstool
(Needs a lamp.)
A pumpkin bungalow
(Warm but damp.)
A robin's nest
(With garden views)
A pond-side mushroom
(Boat to use.)
A giant's shoe
(May need repairs.)
A rabbit's burrow
(Mind the stairs.)

A cosy mouse hole
(Small but cheap.)
A treetop villa
(Rather steep.)
A flowerpot castle
(Cracked by hail.)

Houses for sale!

Houses for Sale!!

The Fairy Queen

Clare found this poem inside a beautiful bird's nest

The Fairy Queen is so gentle,
So very quiet.

Her songs are softer than owl feathers,
And her little feet
In their shiny green hunting boots
Seem as light as dandelion seeds.

Yet the two fearsome Stag Beetles
Who guard her throne
Trot after her like puppies,
And hungry birds with hooked beaks
Build nests for her
In high places.
Even the wasps bring her presents
Wrapped in home-made paper.

For there is power
In her dark, brown eyes,
And all her words
Are true
And wise.

The Fairy in the Bathroom

Clare found this poem underneath her plastic duck

There's a fairy in our bathroom.
She isn't dressed in pink,
She wears a stripy swimsuit,
She splashes round our sink,
She does a little tap dance,
She flaps her water wings,
She dangles from the soap dish,
She bungee-jumps. And sings.

She's soaked the mats and towels,
She hasn't finished yet –
And that is why it's NOT MY FAULT
The floor is dripping wet.

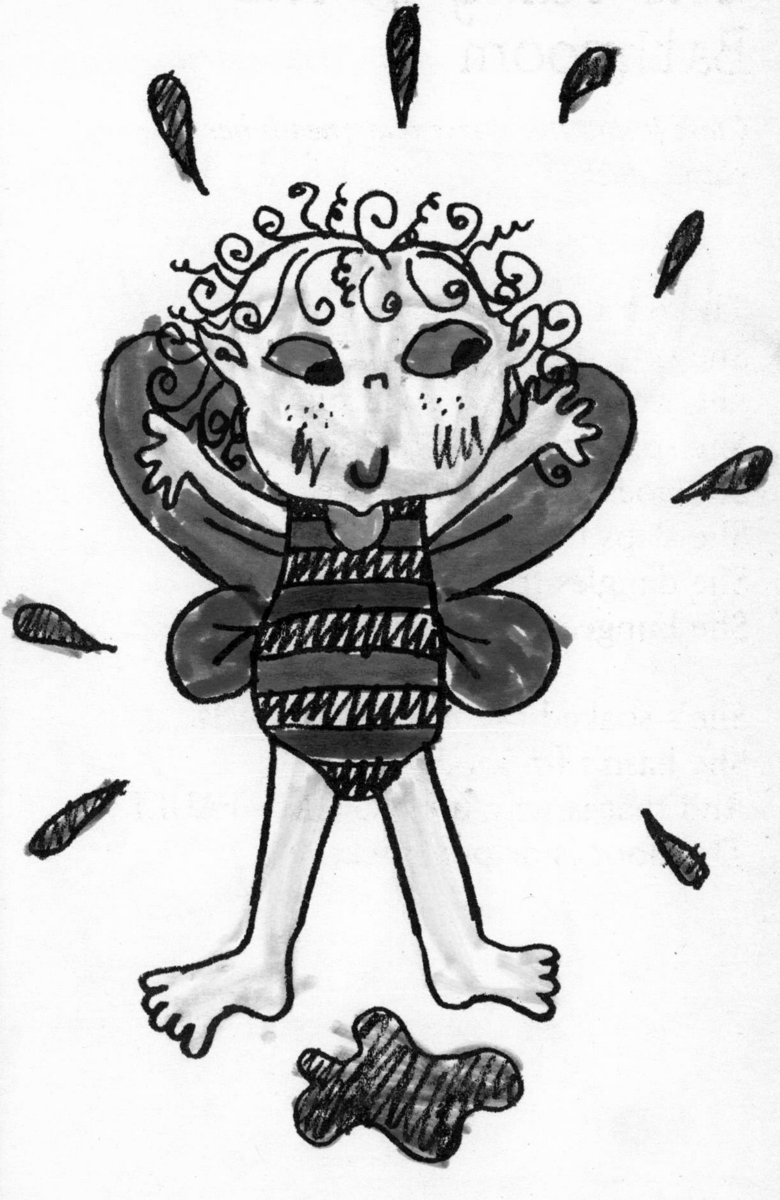

Adverts

Scribbled on stones in Clare's garden

BUY OUR GLOW-WORMS
Tame and bright,
Just the thing
For party night.

FROGSKIN SLIPPERS
Soft and green.
as worn by our
Fairy Queen.

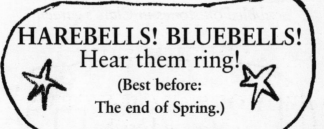

HAREBELLS! BLUEBELLS!
Hear them ring!
(Best before:
The end of Spring.)

SPOTTY TOADSTOOLS

Watch them grow
In a circle,
Not a row.

SPIDER SILK
Freshly spun.
Dive and dangle –
Have some fun!

LEAF-BOARDS FOR SALE!
Leap through the trees.
*We sell acorn helmets
And moss for your knees.*

Other wands wave.
Other wands shake.
But

OUR WANDS SPARKLE!
And NEVER break.

The Lost Fairy

Clare found this poem in a small, sandy bucket

When the sun came up
The lost fairy grew frightened.

What would happen if a human child
    caught her?
Would she be kept in a glass jar
Like a goldfish?
Would she be tied on a string,
And made to fly in endless circles?
Would she be teased? Or squeezed?
Or accidentally squashed?

She curled inside a small, sandy bucket
In a strange corner of the park
And trembled.

When the human child found her,
He placed her gently on his shoulder
And carried her beyond
The sandpit and the pond,
The climbing frame and the fountain

And the park keeper's tidy garden
To her own, friendly tree.
Now he set her
Carefully, carefully down
And trudged away
Without asking for a single wish.

But a little of her magic
Must have dusted his
        fingers,

Because when he
        reached home
There, on the doorstep,
Sat dear old Barker
Who had been missing
        many days,
And now ran to meet him
With a happy, doggy grin.

How to Make Fairy Dust

This poem just blew through Clare's open window

Skitter, scatter
Starry sparks
Over towns
And woods
And parks.
Wait for three
Enchanted hours,
Gather blue
And purple
Flowers,
Shake their
Powder
In the cup
Of an acorn,
Stir it up
With a whisker
From a kitten.

Do EXACTLY
As I've written,
Let the magic
Glint and grow,
(Not too fast and
Not too slow.)
Now you may and
Now you must
Skitter, scatter
Fairy Dust.

How to Use Fairy Dust

This poem just fluttered into Clare's litter-bin

Sprinkle on the sad
(You'll make them happy.)
Sprinkle on the cross.
(They won't be snappy.)
Sprinkle on the weak.
(They'll soon be strong.)
Sprinkle on the shy.
(They'll sing a song.)
Sprinkle on the bad.
(They might be good.)
Sprinkle on the scared.
(I think you should.)
Sprinkle on the clouds.
(You'll see the sun.)
Sprinkle on a birthday cake.
(It's time for FUN!)

The Song of the Naughty Fairies

Clare heard someone singing this on the first day of April

Let's be naughty,
Let's have fun,
Let's play tricks
On EVERYONE.

We'll blow away wigs,
Put wings on the pigs,
Turn cats into dogs,
Paint flowers on frogs,
Teach fishes to sing,
Let spiders go PING,
Draw a smile on the sun,
Make tortoises RUN,
Make hedgehogs all cuddly,
Make neat things all muddly,
Make socks disappear,
Hang hats on the deer,
Give tigers pink spots,

Tie snakes into knots,
Hide a whale in the pool,
Send rabbits to school,
Break EVERY rule . . .

Then we'll shout,
"APRIL FOOL!!"

Ten Fairy Facts

☆The Fairy King's favourite food is Chestnut Chips.

☆The Fairy Queen's favourite pet is a green beetle called "Sprout".

☆The Bad Fairy's favourite spell is "Turning Sweet Things Salty".

☆This year, the two most popular names for new fairies are: Comet-Rider (Boys) and Magpie (Girls).

☆ The most popular wand is made from stolen Christmas decorations.

☆ The most popular flying shoes have bat-leather wings.

☆ The most popular home is a bird's nest lined with cat fur.

☆ The most popular game is Leaf-Boarding.

☆The most popular toy is the Rocking Horse-Fly.

☆The most popular helmet is a spiky conker case, cut in half and lined with spider silk.

Fairy Jokes

Clare Bevan says that fairies find these terribly funny

☆ What is a fairy's favourite lesson at school?
★ Spelling.

☆ What do fairies eat at parties?
★ Fairy cakes, of course.

☆What sound does a fairy's doorbell
  make?
★Wing!

☆What sound does a fairy's mobile phone
  make?
★Wing, wing, wing!

☆What sound does a fairy make when she
  sneezes?
★A-wish-ooo!

☆What illness do fairies catch at
  Christmas?
★Tinsellitis.

☆What do you call a fairy who likes waving?
★**Wanda.**

☆Twinkle, twinkle!
★**Who's there?**
☆Wanda.
★**Wanda who?**
☆I Wanda where that fairy went?

And finally – a birthday joke . . .

☆Twinkle, twinkle!
★**Who's there?**
☆A fairy.
★**A fairy who?**
☆A fairy-happy-birthday to YOU!

Toothpaste Trouble

**Poems from Breakfast to Bedtime
chosen by Nick Toczek**

A brilliant, lively collection of poems to take
you through a day in your life.

Why Are You Late for School?

I didn't get up
because I was too tired
and I was too tired
because I went to bed late
and I went to bed late
because I had homework
and I had homework
because the teacher made me
and the teacher made me
because I didn't understand
and I didn't understand
because I wasn't listening
and I wasn't listening
because I was staring out of the window
and I was staring out of the window
because I saw a cloud.
I am late, sir,
because I saw a cloud.

Steve Turner

Wizard Poems

Magical verses, rhymes and spells
chosen by Fiona Waters

A marvellous, mighty, mystical and magical collection
packed with interesting characters like the Wizard of
Northlands, a not very willing wizard who has put a
spell on himself. Abracadabra!

The Wizard's Book

If you want to read his Spell Book
You must take it by surprise . . .

It watches from the bookshelf
With its fierce and inky eyes
It hears your softest footfall
With its folded paper ears,
It sniffs your fear like perfume,
And it feeds on children's tears.

It lurks in dust and shadows
Where it waits for musty ages
To trap your prying fingers
In its swift and vicious pages,
It tempts you with its secrets
It lures the quick and clever

It lets you think you've won the game
The snap – you're lost forever!

Clare Bevan

A selected list of titles available from Macmillan Children's Books

The prices shown below are correct at the time of going to press. However, Macmillan Publishers reserves the right to show new retail prices on covers which may differ from those previously advertised.

The Monster Who Ate the Universe	0 330 41523 9	£4.99
Poems by Roger Stevens		
The Dog Ate My Bus Pass	0 330 41800 9	£3.99
Poems chosen by Nick Toczek & Andrew Fusek Peters		
Spectacular Schools	0 330 39992 6	£3.99
Poems chosen by Paul Cookson & David Harmer		

All Pan Macmillan titles can be ordered from our website, www.panmacmillan.com, or from your local bookshop and are also available by post from:

**Bookpost,
PO Box 29, Douglas, Isle of Man IM99 1BQ**

Credit cards accepted. For details:
Telephone: 01624 677237
Fax: 01624 670923
E-mail: bookshop@enterprise.net
www.bookpost.co.uk

Free postage and packing in the United Kingdom